A LOAD OF MULLARKEY

A LOAD OF MULLARKEY

HUGH MULLARKEY

Paper Doll

©Hugh Mullarkey, 1998

First Published in 1998 by
Paper Doll
1 Hutton Close
South Church
Bishop Auckland
Durham

ISBN : 1 86248 026 5

Typeset and Printed by
Lintons Printers, County Durham.

*Dedication : To all who have helped
and supported me.*

CONTENTS

DON'T YOU TRY TO POETIZE ME!

Just you be careful
Or I will write
A verse or two about you!
Just you watch out!
Don't you try to versify me
You anapaestic little ditty.

Don't give me none of that
Dactylic backchat neither
If you don't want to find yourself in verse
Or worse.
You'll end up like some
Lousy doggerel
So you will.

Don't you give me none of that
Sonnet stuff neither.
Fourteen lines
And you're anybody's
And yet you couldn't rhyme
Or scan a limerick.

I suppose you'll scazon off
And go and haiku
Some poor old lady
Or something
I'll give you seventeen syllables
So stick that in your pentameter
Iambic or not.
You're positively metaphysical.

I've had it up to here
With your nutty couplets too.
When Laurie ate some
With his prose
He prosified his prosody
And ended up quite onomatopoeic.

You wouldn't know a trochee
From a troica
And as for rhythm
You've gone a foot
Too far too often.
Don't give me none of those
Blank verses neither.
Compose yourself.

You'll be the first to elegize
When I am gone.
Well you can keep your
Silly stanzas
To yourself
I've got a quatrain to catch.

SPARE A THOUGHT

When a thought tried to enter his head
He couldn't believe what it said.
It pleaded with him:
'Won't you please let me in -
If the Internet catch me I'm dead.'

DOES IT NEED TO BE SAID?

Does it fill you with utter dismay
That whatever you're trying to say
The beginning of night
Is nowhere in sight
You are stuck 'at the end of the day'.

FATHER GERARD

The strongest man I ever knew.
His strength lay in the silence
That gives us pause.
He shared his strength with me
And I am ever in his debt.

UTTER PERFECTION

Do you remember that childhood break of day -
A latent stillness of dewy greens and blues
Waiting for the first touch of fire from the sun?

The piquant picture that presents itself
Appealing to every sense that lies receptive
To the magic that you can't define.

The sweet cacophony of rival songs,
The potent purity of pleasure that it brings
That makes you wish that it would never change

But that like all things human
As the clock of life moves on
It is the transitory nature of the memory
That lingers still.

STANDING IN

Apparently my friend Bill has got the flu
Struck down last night or so it seems.
Anyway I've got to take his lesson with 4X
A charming group of youngsters, keen as mustard
To destroy anybody's efforts to impress
A little learning on their vacant brains.

Standing in at lessons is like standing out
Outstanding as a target or fair game.
A chance for all the class to prove their mettle
And show their need for status in each other's
    eyes.
Every one of them will try to show they're leader
    of the pack.
I've got them for a double, wish me luck!

Now Bill won't have had the time to set them
    work
The video's not available - broken down
Another minor problem - I'm no biologist at all
To cap it all this form don't know me well.
They have a reputation to maintain.
If they're feeling fractious then I'm stymied so to
    speak.

It starts superbly. Orchestrated with
Such subtlety and gently overwhelming skill.
One girl far right: 'What do you want us to do -
    Sir?'

One boy far left: 'Sir didn't set us any work -
    Sir'.
Another girl centre front: 'Perhaps he's having
    trouble - Sir. Do you think he's stuck?'
Another boy centre back: 'In a traffic jam of
    course or got a puncture - can't find his jack'.

'I'm sorry you lot. You'll just have to find a book
    to read'.
The moans, the echoes start, rising slowly in pitch
    and volume now.
It's punctuated by quadraphonic interjections of
    all sorts:
'I ain't got no something book!' - 'Here, I'll lend
    you this. Look out!'
'Can't you read something to us - Sir?' 'Yes, go
    on - Sir, I love stories.'
'We're supposed to be doing reproduction - Sir!'

And so it goes on relentlessly
Distraction to the left of me, distraction to the
    right of me
All timed and sequenced to perfection.
You can feel yourself start to simmer,
Then to boil in sheer frustration. It's out of hand.
The longest eighty minutes in anybody's life.

GET YOU ON!

The horses have bolted.
The old stable door
Is completely unhinged
On the mucky old floor.
The turkeys just gobble
Then gobble some more
With the rats and the mice
And the chickens galore.
The farmer tries vainly
To muster his flocks
While adorning his feet
With malodorous socks.
With wellies akimbo
And elbows astride
He shouts to his wife
That the ferret has died.
He girds up his loins
And distributes his weight
When the tractor is mounted
He'll drive through the gate.
He'll milk all the cows
Put the pigs in the trough
Tell the ducks not to quack
Tell the goose not to cough.
He'll shovel manure
When the harvesting's done
Then muck out the stable
And pigsty for fun.
When his Missis
Shouts something

That jest might be lunch
He'll stop what he's doing
Swing a gret old big punch
When he swallows a sausage
Too hot for a munch
'Get you on me old beauty'
He'll yell in her ear.
'Don't you frimmock and garp at me.
Lord do you look queer
You gret Bishee-Barnabee
Bigoty hean
Don't jest dingle and dawdle
Like a gret harvest-queen.'
Later that day Mrs Farmer
Had to lie down with one of her heads.

'Get you on!'

The 'Get You On' Glossary
Get you on = Get you on.
Gobble = Turkeyspeak.
Cough = The goose has an audibly challenged

                                                    hiss.

Jest = Jest or Just.
Gret = Of considerable dimensions - big.
Frimmock = To give oneself airs.
Garp = To stare.
Bishee-Barnabee = Ladybird.
Bigoty = Self-opinionated.
Hean = Mature female chicken.
Dingle = Move slowly and awkwardly.
Dawdle = Move slowly thus being awkward.
Get you on = Get you on.

DEPRESSION

One of life's loose cannons
Which seemingly secure
Will slowly run amok
Remorselessly
As frame by frame
You watch.

Criticisms implied
Or stated or imagined -
The nagging doubts
That importune -
The enemy within
Besieges from without
And expectations of disappointment
Verging on self-pity
Chip away.

Action taken
Bounces back
Rebounding not redounding
Confounding intention with result.

As a puppet
In the hands of fate
You try to pull yourself together
But cannot move.

That's when you need some faith
Some love to give some hope.
Resurrection's tough -
Don't fight alone.

BY APPOINTMENT - WHIPPING BOY

Who is the Prince in your life?
Who lets you take the rap?
Who is all smiles and innocence
While you bear the major brunt? -
The goat of his escape.

Have no fear, we all know that presence,
That passer of the king-sized buck.
His Highness makes the rules for us.
His Highness is always right behind us
Laughing up our sleeves.

He clings to us like limpet burrs -
A parasite in all but name -
He siphons off respect we need
To keep our sorry dignity.
The haunting reptile that we know so well.

He is a master of disguise/deceit.
We're witness to his every act.
Apparently kind and gracious, he
Just leads us on and on and on.
We are his stepping-stones and slaves.

Please do not worry, it's of no avail.
You're in attendance: at his summons,
Swimming in a vat of treacle persecution.
Freedom is the one thing that he can never give.
As you are subservient to his needs and ploys.
For Prince and Boy read Person too.

PUT YOUR SPELLING TO THE TEST

A dry list of listless sounds
That are the recipe for tomorrow's disaster:
The spelling test.

The importance of the groups of letters
Is not now in their subtle shades
Of meaning,

But in their combinations so to speak!
The underwear of all vocabulary:
The spelling test.

The league tables of literature.
The components of our language now deprived
Of meaning.

'Eight out of twenty - disappointing!
Last week you got eleven. You must improve.'
The spelling test.

And yet without this charmless knowledge
We couldn't even find our goal
Of meaning.

The alphabet alone is not the key
To dictionaries and directories.
The spelling test

Will help us find our way
Along all those routes and branches
Of meaning.

Contest it, detest it, of interest
Divest it: that necessary evil:
The spelling test.

BUT MUM....!

Although there's always a lot of growing up
    going on,
There's always a lot of children around too -
Or perhaps alot and not a lot -
If you - know what I mean?

A lot of rubble, glass and shrapnel
Old torn toys and fractured pictures
A lot of faded family photos no longer really
    framed
But torn and curly where the water's been
And gone and left a desert where once was
    priceless love
And now is just a sad memorial that no one
    knows or understands.

But wait - some life would seem to stir!
A tentative scrabbling can be heard.
A sudden cry as one small figure
Lurches into view grazing a pile of wreckage
While it grazes him or her -
Difficult to tell with all that
Dirt and dust and damage.

What was once a boring house
You never noticed as you passed
Was now an Aladdin's cave.
It didn't matter what was there.
What mattered now was more what might be
there.

'Don't you go near them bombed-out houses
Dear. All them rusty nails and things
You rip that shirt - we can't get another
Anyway you'll soon be back at school
When they can find a hall or somefink.
You go and play on the common
Somewhere sensible and safe
And take young Jo(e)....'

'But Mum.....!'

'Don't you 'but' me!
You do as you're told for once,
I don't want some warden
Telling me you found a UXB.
And wasn't wiv us no more.'

'But Mum.....!'

'You get along now
And stay out of them shelters.
Give a good example for once in your life
I've got to go to work.'

'But Mum......!'

But that was that.
Now for a bit of serious exploring.

'Jo(e)! Jo(e)! Where are you?
Jo(e)?'

Another scrabble, another smaller cry
This time from behind another heap
Of fallen masonry and wood.

'Come on Jo(e).
Stop foolin' round.
You're always spoilinevryfink.'

The nasty noise of folding brickwork
Makes exploration stop
And fear run wild.

SEEN IT ALL BEFORE

At the end of the day -
When all's said and done.
When the end is away
And your duty is done
What's in it for you?
What's in it for me?
Don't give me that excrement!
Know what I mean?
Just don't grass me up.
Don't squeal to me mates
Or the filth and blaggers
That work this estate.
Give me some ecstasy.
Give us a kiss.
In life's great big disco
You've gotta find bliss.
Never responsible,
Never alone.
Freak out and fix it.
You're turning to stone.

A CHAT ABOUT LIFE

Can we be sure who gave us life?

What a stupid question!

It's not in doubt - it's <u>biological</u>!

Isn't it?

No, what I mean is life, not - life!

Oh.

Can we give it back?

What, when you're fed up with it you mean?

No, give it back.

Yes you kick the bucket - didn't you know - didn't
    anybody tell..

I know we didn't ask for it in the first place - but..

But what?

You know.

Know what?!

What I mean..

Look..

You may not have asked for it..

I got that..

Well you don't ask for prezzies do you?

Eh?

You don't actually ask for prezzies do you?

What about lists - wedding presents and things?

Now you're being awkward.

Look - what are you on about?

Life is just a bowl of prezzies or somefink?

When you get a prezzie you usually want to give
    something back!

Don't you?

True - I suppose...(Some sort of interruption
    occurs.)

TASTE

Taste the verb
And taste the noun.
Tasteful adjectives
Abound.
Tastily season
Verbs and sound.
Taste in every sense
Profound.
Smack your lips
And kiss the ground.
Budding tastes
Just must be found.
Tastefully tasting
Tastes that crown
Culinary smells that
Whisk around
Teasingly, temptingly
Tummy bound.
Fetch every taster!
Let the flavour resound.
Tastelessness banished
From life's merry-go-round.

GOOD TASTE

Culture, taste,
Or contempt of same,
Is classified,
As upper or lower
Class by name.

Can you imagine,
A world so free
Of rooted prejudice
That we
Can talk to one another
And just be
Just as people -
Status-free?

Just as people,
You and me.

HINDSIGHT

The posters paint the pictures
In your troubled mind:
'Come and live in hindsight
And all solutions find!'
It would seem to be in hindsight
All problems disappear.

With a patronising look at you
All hindsight people state:
'I could have told you that my friend.'
The catchphrase that you hate
If you're just looking for advice
You'll have it never fear.

Then you decide that hindsight
Will give you what you seek
You emigrate to save yourself and end up up the
      creek.
'I told you so, I told you so.'
Is the language that they speak.

You went to live in hindsight
To find your future there
No one's around, there's not a sound
You only find despair.
Go back to where your future starts
Then for that you can prepare.

MR GLIB?

You want your cake and eat it,
Said the wise man to his son.
You can't change the rules to suit yourself
You can't just have all the fun
Somewhere, somehow as you arrive
You'll catch yourself coming back.
You'll still be searching for ecstasy
While buying up loads of crack
You'll see ahead with deja vu
And wish you were not there
'Cos there's nothing in life that you can take
That's better than just taking care.

IT'S CRIMINAL!

'I thought I'd look you up' said Jim
As he looked him up and down.
'It's been a long time
Since that hideous crime
I'm arresting you now Mr Brown.

I'll give you a nice proper caution
That anything that you do say
May be strong evidence
And it ain't no defence
To make out that it isn't fair play.

So come quietly now - be a good boy!
You really must try to come clean.
If you want to confess
To your known guiltiness
Then we might try to just intervene.

So that when My Lord Judge gives his verdict
And your sentence comes to be passed
You'll get three years not more
Not the full twenty-four
Your parole will be granted so fast

That you'll hardly have time to get used to
Your nice little cell in block 'L'
Before you find your feet
You'll be out on the street
Not banged up with some monster from hell.'

Like a fool Mr Brown pleaded 'guilty'
Then the Home Secretary got wind
Of his desperate ploy
And reacted - oh boy
He couldn't wait for a chance to rescind

Anybody who tried to pass sentence
That was less than a lifetime or two
Was served with a writ
Forced to grovel and quit
Then locked in a cell with no loo.

INVASION OF THE ISOPODS!

They don't have the decency
The ones in my hall
To try the disguise
Of a miniature ball

Whether creepies or crawlies
They scuttle or glide
'Cross the floor, up the walls
Gravitation defied

Under paths under buildings
Under foot as I speak
They lurk and they loiter
All armoured and sleek

Where they think they're entitled
To occupy space
They invade and infest
Every new hiding place

The woodlice are coming
Hurray and hurrah
As they trundle then gridlock
Then park like a car

As we watch them manoeuvre
From our vantage point high
Like a video camera
In a rotor-filled sky

We will see how they drive us
To distraction dismay
But we can't stamp them out
Or even drive them away.

CORPORAL EDUCATION

Agitato dominie,
Ye gods and little fish!
When will they try to understand
It is my dearest wish
To impress upon their wandering minds
That effort is required:
That progress only can be made
When progress is desired

That ablatives are absolute
That grammar rules OK
That if they'd worked pluperfectly
In subjunctive mood let's say
Their problems would be over
And running in their blood
Would be the guts of every primer
Taken at their flood.

But ah! There was a better answer -
To such stress and strain.
A different tale when I was able
To wield my trusty cane
To thrash a little knowledge
Into all their stubborn minds
So that they could soak up knowledge
By way of sore behinds.

Thus through their seats of learning
By magic it would seem
They'd fulfil their parents' yearnings
Beyond their wildest dreams.
They'd all sign up for Mensa
All ignorance would flee.
The proof is here before your eyes:
It did no harm to me!

GRACE LACKADAY IS HEARING
THINGS AGAIN

Grace Lackaday is cast away.
Her island, once her home,
Repels all boarders and yet
Does rigid borders fabricate -
She fortifies her isolation thus.
Grace Lackaday is hearing things again.

While confusion grows within
Without it embraces all.
How do we help?
Self-segregation deters approach.
What she needs she does not want
And yet her very want of company
Wants fellowship and love.
Grace listens but she does not hear.

The lifelines are rejected
By her pride.
Her would-be rescuers can only watch
As the sharks of her imagination
Eat away her life.
Grace Lackaday is lost. At sea.

The slow remorseless breakdown
Of a mind and soul
Which can seem self-inflicted
Wear and tear
Shows to all of us, the horrifying
Frailty of life
We can watch it happening before our eyes.
Grace Lackaday as time runs out.

And yet we are involved.
The vortex of senility
Engrosses us, engulfs
With no apparent reason
Discernible or right.
Grace Lackaday is lost and losing more each day.

It brings a sense of guilt
About something we have done
Or maybe failed to do.
Perhaps we knew the lifeline
That we threw
Was frayed and brittle.
Perhaps we didn't bother.
Grace Lackaday can drown herself.

Does one bother oneself to save a nuisance or a bane?
If not - Why not?
You are troubled to justify
Your thoughts and actions to yourself.
Grace Lackaday has cast herself away.

She is deaf to all of us
Alone except for the loving care
Of her two cats - one black, one white.
If only life could be so simple!
She talks to them
And they talk back.
They give her something that she seeks.
Grace Lackaday is one with them.

Self-preservation
Can be cruel
And love thy neighbour
As thyself
A broken rule.
Grace Lackaday is incompatible and strange.

And so Grace Lackaday withdraws
And tries to rally her command.
She will remain within her keep.
No bailey left.
In her imagination enemies encroach.
Grace Lackaday is under siege.

Give in. Give up without a fight.
Make peace not war.
The enemy you fight
Can never be defeated
Lies within.
Grace Lackaday is hearing things again.

THE TEACHER

Everybody knows better than the teacher.
Ofsted! Ofsted! We all fall down.
The importance of your pupils is
Greater than the sum of all your efforts.

Why do the pupils make them all blind?
The open door, that open you find,
Opens onto a tightly closed mind.

For all we are about to receive
And all that came before.
Give us the stress and we'll finish your job.
It's all to do with tricks of the confidence
You've always shown in us in every way.

Light the blue touch-paper and then retire!
But wait till you're old enough.
Stay stoke the fire
Until all that glows is blown away.

Governors and government,
All govern us with great intent.
All see themselves as heaven-sent
Slow down and think!
Then give us back our jobs.

FOR HEAVEN'S SAKE REST IN PEACE

At the end of the day when you're dead,
We will hopefully all hear it said,
You were such a good friend
That you lived to the end
And were never alone in your bed.

LOOKING AFTER ME MUM!

Me Mother's minder is me.
I'm her stout major domo you see,
At her beck or her call
Whether kitchen or hall
I'm wherever she needs me to be.

DO YOU EVER GET THE FEELING...?

Excuse me I'm looking for offence.
Looking for a fence?
That's right.
What is it then -
Stolen goods
Or lack of privacy?
Are you trying to be funny?
Well I'm obviously not succeeding -
If I am.
There's no need to take that tone with me!
I'm sorry -
I'm only trying to help -
Why do you want a fence?
I beg your pardon?
Why do you want a fence?
I see -
You are deliberately misunderstanding me.
Eh?
You are making a silly pun
In order to cause me embarrassment.
What do you mean?
Some people seem to find humour
In mockery and humiliation.
You can't be serious! (slight chortle.)
There you go again.
Eh?
Since the beginning of this lamentable conversation
You have done nothing but
Belittle and ridicule -
You should be ashamed of yourself -

It's people like you
That are dragging this country down.
Look I...
Oh it's no good pretending
You didn't mean it -
They all do that -
You think it's so clever...
I'm sorry but...
It's no good apologising now -
The damage is done -
You are an utter disgrace!
I'm sorry, I don't think you understand.
Oh it's me that doesn't understand now -
Is it?
That's right it's always someone else's fault -
Never you.
Honestly, I was only trying to help.
There you go again:
'I was only trying to help.' -
It's people like you that make
Muggers look like charity workers.
Now it's you that's being offensive.
Oh it's me now is it?
That's right -
Walk away -
That proves it doesn't it?
Where are your clever answers now?
Off you go -
Back to your little friends -
No wonder the world's in the state it's in now -
You're all the same -
You people...

WHEN TIME SLOWS

Waiting in life's waiting room
Decision made
Now consequences loom
On the horizon of your mind

Treading water time does lag
The hand of fate
Will ultimately drag
You so irrevocably on

Right before your very eyes
Beyond control
It comes as no surprise
Yet somehow shocks you to the core

'Wait and see.' You wait and hear
You bide your time
But deep inside you fear
You wish that you need never know

Pessimistic thoughts that thrive
And eat away
The instinct to survive
Are cancers of the spirit too

They could bring you to despair
That would be wrong
Is all beyond repair?
Don't put yourself beyond all hope

Listen to that voice inside
You, mark it well
You've been preoccupied
You need to find yourself again.

HITLER HAD ONLY GOT ONE CAUSE

Wanted, wanted, wanted,
Somebody else's toys
If you cannot have them straight away:
Destroy, destroy, destroy.

It has got to be fair on your terms
As you see it let it be.
Fate owes you that
It is written
It is your sweet destiny.

Let's all go a-coveting
To take what should be ours.
If you cannot have the garden
Then trample down the flowers.

It's your right and it's your duty
As you go about your work
To tempt and bribe and then coerce
Lest your minions
Start to shirk.

Don't think in terms of complex
Don't listen to such talk
You cannot build an empire
While they babble and they baulk.

It's a sign of your success you know
That they rally and they roar.
Accept their loyal worship
You are not a man
Of straw.

But then like every empire
Where domineering is the rule
Eventually the idol will
Fall to be the fool.

It is tragic to see a people
Led by an hysterical urge
Make history by the tumbril
They can never hope to purge.

A PURGATORY POEM

Clinical depression!
What a sheer relief to know it has a name.
Perhaps, now, it will be possible to come to terms
Although a desert island is where I am.

Don't be despondent anyone.
You will have to let me be.
What in your eyes will seem unreasonable,
Selfish, stubborn, resentful, unpredictable and sad.

If I am in a sorry state and self-pity seems to rule
My life, I can't explain it - how I wish I could.

It's as if the blame for every ill is mine:
The voice that whispers in my ear:
'You'll get it wrong. You know you will.
It's rubbish and you know it is.'

'Don't tell me that you mean it well.
You're not worth knowing are you?
By trying to do the right thing you offend.
Give up and hide. Just disappear.'

'I despise you. You have my full contempt.'

A long, slow, tortuous climb; with treatment,
With counsellors who listen - don't dismiss.
A roller-coaster of hope and of despair
That one day will lift the clouds.

MYSTERIOUS WAYS

We have our own mysterious ways
Our wonders to perform.
We have those grand idyllic days,
The sunshine proud and warm.

We feel alive. We feel inspired.
We know we're not alone.
Love requited. Love desired.
The love that we have known.

There is a power, a driving force
From without us yet inside.
We are fulfilled, an endless source
Of joy and simple pride.

Take comfort. Take a look at life.
Take time to take a rest,
To look around and see yourself
At your very very best.

WHAT COMPROMISES COMPROMISE?

Under what circumstances
Do you live?
What controls?
Tell me you know the answer
To every question posed.

Life's intractable attrition
Can yet reduce
The solid citizen
Who stands alone
And cannot contemplate another's way.

Surely an opinion
That cannot change
Is brittle, fragile,
Vulnerable too -
No room to manoeuvre or escape.

When your mistakes
Follow doggedly in your wake
They dog your days
And beg attention
Demanding that you make allowance now.

WHO'S REVOLTING NOW?

Find a cause, find an issue,
Find a reason to pursue
Any hobbyhorse and faction
That can appeal to you.

Dig a tunnel, climb a tree,
Make a protest, do feel free
To indulge in degradation
To aggravate aggressively.

Just lay waste to human values
Be revolting, join the cruise -
Name your own ship the *Titanic*
Sink the world and make the news.

From your litter literally
Find fulfilment - anarchy!
Don't accept imposed restrictions
Don't look back or you might see.

NO RESERVE

At an auction
I attended
Packed among
The folks who bid
I listened - all
Belief suspended
As the chatter
Rose and fell.

The auctioneer
Began his onslaught
Always prefaced
By the words
'It'll serve its purpose.'
Then the gavel
Then the gabble
Rose and fell.

'It'll serve its purpose'
Give me five
Make me a better offer
Keep the rotten bid alive
Parting people
From their money
As excitement
Rose and fell.

Rose and Felicity
Want a washstand
Maude wants teapots -

Not for tea
Lionel fancies
A box of trinkets
As his eyelid
Rose and fell.

Now the pace
Is getting frantic
Two stuffed budgies
Are going cheap
There's a new
Electric blanket
Bidders' hands just
Rose and fell.

'Can I have a proper bid please'
'It really is quite nice'
'It'll serve its purpose'
'This Victorian novelty'
'Therapeutic good vibrations'
He made sounds that
Rose and fell.

Now the bidding
For a Georgian
Table starts
To gather way
Will it ever
Serve its purpose?
Expectations
Rose and fell.

Then an unstuffed
Mouldy sofa
Then a fractured
Vase or two
All will serve some
Unknown purpose
Car-boot prices
Rose and fell.

The auctioneer
Has served his purpose
Served his bidders
And his boss
And now
The final item
As the hubbub
Rose and fell.

PERCY GOAT, DIED 19TH JANUARY 1915

What a very strange name to find on a bomb
And not even as old as the century was long

What a very strange way for a bomb to arrive
For a boy to be dead and not young and alive

Now all that remains is a small marble cross
Standing sadly neglected such a token of loss

He wasn't a hero, a person of note
But he died for his country did young Percy Goat

Now almost forgotten in our cynical haste
To ignore all the losing, the grief and the waste

Of a century stricken, a time so obscene
It can contemplate killing a boy of fourteen

His death is a symbol of the cheapness of life
In an age where great progress has created great
$$\text{strife}$$

For he died in his home when a Zeppelin made
An apparently brief indiscriminate raid

Thus ushering in a new concept of war
That no one was safe, or could afford to ignore

The fact that the air was no longer free
And could deliver its own form of barbarity

Is Percy symbolic of mankind's desire
To hold up destruction, as a thing to admire?

Too young to be 'honoured', too young to be
    'brave'
Young Percy lies wasted, alone in his grave.

*Percy Goat was the first 'child' to be killed in an
air raid on this country. His death was caused by
a bomb dropped from a Zeppelin on King's Lynn.
The raid took place on 19th January 1915 and
was carried out by Zeppelin L.4.*